Soul Unfinished

FINDING HAPPINESS, TAKING RISKS, & TRUSTING GOD AS WE GROW OLDER

Robert Atwell

WITH A FOREWORD BY EMILIE GRIFFIN

PARACLETE PRESS
BREWSTER, MASSACHUSETTS

Soul Unfinished: Finding Happiness, Taking Risks, and Trusting God as We Grow Older

2012 First Printing

Copyright © 2012 by Robert Atwell

ISBN: 978-1-61261-236-2

Originally published in the UK under the title *The Contented Life* by the Canterbury Press of 13a Hellesdon Park Road, Norwich, Norfolk NR6 5DR and Americanized for this edition.

Library of Congress Cataloging-in-Publication Data

Atwell, Robert.
  Soul unfinished : finding happiness, taking risks, and trusting God as we grow older / Robert Atwell ; with a foreword by Emilie Griffin.
     p. cm.
  Includes bibliographical references.
  ISBN 978-1-61261-236-2
  1. Older people—Religious life. 2. Aging—Religious aspects—Christianity. I. Title.
  BV4580.A89 2012
  248.8'5—dc23   2012027445

10 9 8 7 6 5 4 3 2 1

Published by Paraclete Press
Brewster, Massachusetts
www.paracletepress.com
Printed in the United States of America

CONTENTS

AUTHOR'S NOTE

This book began as a lecture to a group of older people in the Diocese of Chester who felt sidelined by our culture's obsession with youth and celebrity. "Have we nothing to contribute?" they asked. They were fed up with older people being seen as a problem, rather than an asset. They were equally fed up with endless talk about death and dying. What they wanted to talk about was life and living, and what they could contribute to their local communities.

So it was that I gave a talk on contentment and the gift of years. This was subsequently printed as a series of short articles and posted on the Diocesan website, where it generated a huge correspondence. In over thirty years of ministry, I have never had such a large and overwhelmingly positive response to anything I have written, which led me to believe that the themes I was exploring might merit a wider audience.

I am indebted to those who first laid down the gauntlet and made me think about the challenges and opportunities that confront us as we grow older. I would also like to record my thanks to those whose stories are told in this book. Doubtless they will recognize themselves in spite of my efforts to disguise their identity. I am particularly grateful to Margaret Andrews, Rosemary Spencer, and John Varty, all of whom read a draft of the book and made helpful suggestions.

ROBERT ATWELL

FOREWORD
Toward an Artfulness of Aging

At both ends of life we face eternal questions. When we were younger we focused on the future. We wrestled with life decisions. We read how-to books about them. A few of us were occasionally unhinged by them.

In midlife we wondered, could we trim our dreams to match the practical options we had? What was the best way forward? We worried about making wrong choices. Sometimes the decisions we thought were good came back to haunt us. We struggled to apply the lessons we had learned.

Ultimately, by our later years, we had stretched our understandings of life until the rubber band felt sure to break. We told ourselves that we did not care about growing older. "I'm not buying this book for myself, it's for my aunt," we might say.

"Oh, yes, I have a charming uncle, he loves to read."
But of course, before we let that needy, sometimes
mythical aunt or uncle have a look, we'd plunged
into the text ourselves, starving for a crust of consolation. How will I manage? What will I become?
If I don't have the work or the celebrity I used to
have, what will be left of me?

The later years provide a special challenge. We
know we are expected to slow down. For some of
us, this is a difficult thing to do. It confines and
baffles us. We fight back against it.

Some of us find it hard to let go—of the mana-
gerial roles we had, the jobs we were used to, the
particular delight and status of having achieved,
being the sort of person that others admire and
desire to follow. Our life's work is done, we think.
It's time for the rocking chair. Which may be true,
as far as it goes, but very much to our surprise,
there's one more challenge ahead: the unfinished
soul.

Robert Atwell explores this territory with a keen
sense of authority. As a man of the cloth and a

student of the Christian life he knows and can share the Bible's wisdom. As a bishop, he offers the wisdom of the Christian faith, from his own angle to be sure. But he also dips deeply into the well of ancient wisdom, collected and collective, the straight teaching and knowledge on which so many Christian believers depend. He integrates ancient wisdom with modern experiences—including retirement, ways of living, memories, forgiveness, becoming, and happiness. I treasure the ways that he evokes the Scriptures like elders gathering by the temple gate to offer discernment on these aspects of growing older.

Bishop Atwell is especially good on forgiveness, one of the most important challenges of the later years. He knows the accumulated anger in families, the years of estrangement from friends, from relatives, from church. He knows how to frame the questions. He knows how to help the unfinished soul. He knows how deeply we need to forgive ourselves for what we have done and not done. He knows the heart longs to come home.

Who needs this book? I might ask: Who knows enough not to need this book? Will I, when I am ninety, know so much that I won't need the Lord anymore? Rash thought. Foolish generation. It is clear and simple. The surer our ascent into the blaze of wisdom, the greater our dependence on the Lord.

But here's a caution. There's no way to approach this book if you're not willing to dwell with, and live within, metaphors. Robert Atwell keeps them coming thick and fast. The tool box, the exercise bike, the hike up the mountain trail, the resting in the dark valley, all these come at us and we bat them away, telling ourselves we're far too practical for this poetic stuff. Telling ourselves we're much too grownup to be childlike. Figuring that we know the Bible already, we've consulted it on any number of occasions, we love the life of it, the sound of it, the resonance, the beauty of the royal tone. Atwell wants us to know the Bible, but he also wants us to live the Bible. To probe for the deep heart of it, surrendering to at least one and probably multiple metaphors as part of what we do. And how we grow.

There is a warm and confident practicality in Atwell's teaching. He is the grandparent one always wanted, and the fellow adventurer who understands. He is willing to take his shoes off and rest awhile beside cool streams.

Learn to hope. Learn to dream. Learn to play. And most of all, tell the truth to yourself and others. Stop hiding behind the brilliant facades of a lifetime. Stop letting stereotypes of youth and old age dominate you. Admit your own dishonesties, the things you want to overcome, and will not. Forget them and forgive them and move on.

Put on the sandals of surrender. Walk with Christ. Prepare. Have a good time, but have your lamp ready when he comes. Be at peace. Know love and friendship. When you face trials of any kind, consider it nothing but joy.

Change your heart. Or don't change it, if it's already open and bleeding for grace. Change your heart, because today is your chance. Now is the appointed time, Atwell tells us. There's no time like the present, and time is short. But although the way is hard, it is also easy when God's dwelling place is embedded in our hearts. Christ-life will wrap around us, when we follow the Lord's way, ever so practically, into an uncertain future.

EMILIE GRIFFIN

Soul Unfinished

You never enjoy the world aright till the Sea itself floweth in your veins, till you are clothed with the heavens, and crowned with the stars: and perceive yourself to be the sole heir of the whole world, and more than so, because men are in it who are every one sole heirs as well as you. Till you can sing and rejoice and delight in God, as misers do in gold, and Kings in sceptres, you never enjoy the world.

THOMAS TRAHERNE,
Centuries of Meditations

1
Invitation

One of the great things about the twenty-first century is that most of us can expect to live far longer than our grandparents. Modern medical care and good health permit a quality of life vastly superior to what was possible fifty years ago. Life—at least in the developed world—is now roughly divided into three parts: twenty years of education, forty years of work, followed by twenty or thirty years of leisure. But are we prepared for the opportunity that this represents?

Far from being a grim affair of shrinking horizons, growing older can be an adventure, full of new and exciting possibilities. With the mortgage paid and the children flown the nest, our time is our own. No longer at anyone's beck and call, we are free to do what we like. Cheap air flights make travel to remote parts of the world possible. The University of the

Third Age offers a range of educational opportunities. Fitness programs encourage us to keep supple and trim. All this is a rare luxury compared with the lot of previous generations, and marks us out still further from those who live in poorer parts of the world. Suddenly there is the chance to do things we always dreamed of. T. S. Eliot's words beckon us: "Old men ought to be explorers."[1]

Of course, not everyone is energized by a fresh set of opportunities. The prospect of radical change in the pattern of daily life can generate waves of anxiety. Some find the relentless pace of technological change intimidating. They watch young people quickly master the latest piece of electronic wizardry while they fumble. Others find their confidence undermined by the way in which the values and principles they used to measure success no longer seem to matter to a new generation. Do you fight or capitulate? In a society where losing your looks and growing old is feared it is hard to believe your experience is valued, no matter what the official rhetoric declares. Not surprisingly, many older people feel they no longer have significance.

In some professions age is not a handicap. Lawyers and judges in particular are respected for their accumulated wisdom and experience. Lord Denning, the famous Master of the Rolls, was firing on all cylinders to the end. But they are exceptions to the rule. The fixation of the media with youth and celebrity has the unfortunate effect of sidelining older people, whose voice is often under-represented.

It would be wrong to blame everything on youth culture or the media, but the fact remains that in the past older people were honored and valued, as they still are in many parts of the world. For example, the Bible describes the ancient Hebrew institution of the elders of a town gathering at its gate to take counsel or resolve a dispute. As one of the psalms lyrically has it, "The righteous flourish like the palm tree, and grow like a cedar in Lebanon. They are planted in the house of the LORD; they flourish in the courts of God. In old age they still produce fruit; they are always green and full of sap" (Psalm 92:12–13). It is to our shame that we no longer expect the elderly to produce fruit, let alone be full of sap. But watch out: older people can take the world by surprise.

Mary Wesley did not publish her first novel, *Jumping the Queue*, until she was seventy-one. In 1990, at the age of seventy-two, Nelson Mandela emerged on to the world stage from solitary confinement on Robben Island to become President of the Republic of South Africa. By the sheer force of his personality and integrity, he transformed a nation haunted by years of apartheid into a rainbow coalition of peoples built on mutual respect and forgiveness. In 1958 when the cardinals elected Angelo Roncalli pope, they probably imagined that in choosing an old man of seventy-seven they had a safe candidate who could easily be controlled. In the event, Pope John XXIII turned out to be one of the great reforming popes, determined to throw open the doors of the Church to new ideas. Old men may not only be explorers, they may be revolutionaries.

Take risks

I remember staying with friends when an elderly neighbor came to lunch. Although he was ninety-two and tottered in on two sticks, he was alert and bright as a button. At the end of lunch our host escorted him to the door where a taxi was waiting to take him home. "Well, take care, Bill," he said, holding out his hand. Quick as a flash the old boy spun round. "I'm fed up with people telling me to take care. What I say is 'Take risks!' In fact that's how I end all my letters these days—take risks."

As I grow older the question confronting me is whether I want to end up like Bill or Mr. Grumpy. What sort of person do I wish to be? I have a choice. I can opt to live in the past, nursing my disappointments, and become resentful and embittered. Or I can live in the present with thankfulness, excited by new ideas, enjoying the company of friends and family. And above all, prepared to take risks.

Sharing wisdom

In the sixth century St. Benedict wrote in his monastic *Rule* about the importance of *senpectae*, "of wise old men" in a community. He celebrates the wisdom that can come from having lived a long time. Today more information is available to us than ever before. The Internet provides instant access to rafts of knowledge. We are bombarded with surveys and statistics. But having more information does not necessarily mean we are any wiser. We still need the wisdom of experience to navigate our way. We need the perspective that comes only with maturity.

Sadly, older people today are more likely to be seen as encumbrances to change than reservoirs of wisdom. In my experience it is usually the gray-haired, not the white-haired, the middle-aged as opposed to the elderly, who resist change. Older people are often more tolerant of contradictions and are not fixated about discovering "the right answer" to problems. With less to prove (and lose) they can be remarkably free. Many are open to new things and embrace the younger generation gladly. They can draw upon deep wells of experience and play a significant part in the life of their families and neighborhoods. Time-rich, they often carry their wisdom lightly, but bring ballast and stability to a community.

Many young people have little to do with the elderly, and many older people feel they have nothing to contribute to the aspiring young. This is tragic because they have much to offer, not least sharing the secret of their resilience. Some find fulfilling roles within the network of their families, supporting their hardworking children and providing care for the grandchildren. Others take up positions of responsibility in their community or church, and gain a real sense of fulfillment. Yet others discover a new zest for life working with voluntary organizations or helping children with their reading in local schools. The skills and expertise of older people represent a major resource that needs to be mobilized. Here are two examples.

For the last ten years Christine has worked one day a week on a voluntary basis for a charity dedicated to the rehabilitation of young offenders. Now in her early seventies and still a consummate "multitasker," she juggles tap classes and looking after the grandchildren with mentoring ex-prisoners. She visits them in advance of their release date to build a relationship, and then weekly for three months to help them readjust to "life outside." In the early days of release, she maintains daily contact by mobile phone. This is the crucial time when someone is most likely to drift back into old habits. By her own admission she is "pretty unshockable," and being a volunteer and a woman, she says, helps. "These young men are not nearly as tough as they make out.

Few have enjoyed a stable family life. I'm not sure how they view me; probably somewhere between a friend and the mother they never had. But they can be vulnerable with me."

Derek, a former businessman now in his mid-eighties, acts as a mentor to two disaffected teenagers who are in need of a listening ear. He has been drawn into his church's social inclusion project that seeks to harness the wisdom and time of older citizens to help young people at risk of permanent unemployment, and even prison. He meets them on a one-to-one basis each week during their lunch hour or after school. In his new role of resident uncle, he listens, humors, and advises (for example) how to shape up job applications. He is a calming influence when they get angry. His aim is "to help them discover who they are and to steady them through difficulties." Beneath their youthful cockiness, he says, they surprisingly lack confidence. He feels that the key to success lies in being non-judgmental. Amazingly—or perhaps not—the young people

think Derek is "cool" and have granted him their
ultimate accolade: "respect."

In his poem "Auguries of Innocence," William
Blake was unflinchingly candid about the human
lot:

> Man was made for Joy and Woe,
> And when this we rightly know
> Thro' the World we safely go.

For Blake naiveté is the enemy. Enabling young
people to grow in maturity includes helping them
cope with the shock that bad things can happen
to good people, and that not everyone can win the
race. Sadness and regret are just as much part of
human experience as joy. Growing into adulthood
is not simply about cultivating style or acquiring
skills. It is about learning to deal with shame and
embarrassment, to cope with loss and disappointment, and to find contentment in ordinary things.
Endowing children and young people with the
resources to grasp these insights is a challenge,

but also a wonderful foundation for their future happiness. The question is, how well do we cope with these things ourselves? Are we good role models?

Going deeper

And here lies the spiritual challenge. The last third of life is not just for doing exciting new things. It is also for going deeper into God. Unless we are prepared to grow in spiritual awareness we may end up dissatisfied and restless. Inevitably, as the years pass the accent will fall increasingly on being rather than doing. But this should not matter. When our inner life is kept true, our outer life becomes more fruitful. We may not have the raw energy of a twenty-year-old, but we do have a honed wisdom that comes from experience.

Growing older undoubtedly calls for adjustment. As journalist Richard Needham facetiously puts it, "As you grow old, you lose your interest in sex, your friends drift away, your children often ignore you. There are many other advantages, of course, but these would seem to be the outstanding ones."[2] The pace of life does indeed change. Our health may falter. We may not be so agile or mobile. With the passing of the years we have to reconcile ourselves to the probability that we will not find fulfillment of all our aspirations, but we should still try and honor at least some of them. In novelist E. M. Forster's words, "We must be willing to let go of the life we have planned, so as to have the life that is waiting for us."

There is an art to growing old, and it includes acceptance of ourselves and of our circumstances, at least insofar as they cannot be changed. With a lifetime of experience on which to draw, the challenge is to share our insights without pontificating or becoming a bore. If we succeed, then the joys and disappointments of life will become a toolbox from which we gain wisdom. When we mine the seams of faith and spirituality, we unlock the full potential of this period of our life.

For those ready to grasp it with both hands, our latter years can be one of the most fruitful and rewarding chapters in life. It starts the moment we jettison the negative stereotypes that are thrust on to older people, and celebrate the freedom and opportunities that maturity brings. It entails re-visiting priorities. Above all, it means going deeper into God. A new quality of life can begin at any hour of any day, if we live in the present moment and live wisely.

REFLECTION

If I am to live creatively in the present, I need to reflect on my temperament and outlook, and ask myself some questions:

How can I become more like Bill and less like Mr. Grumpy?

What are the risks I need to take? What can I offer others?

How can I ensure that I am "always green" and "full of sap"?

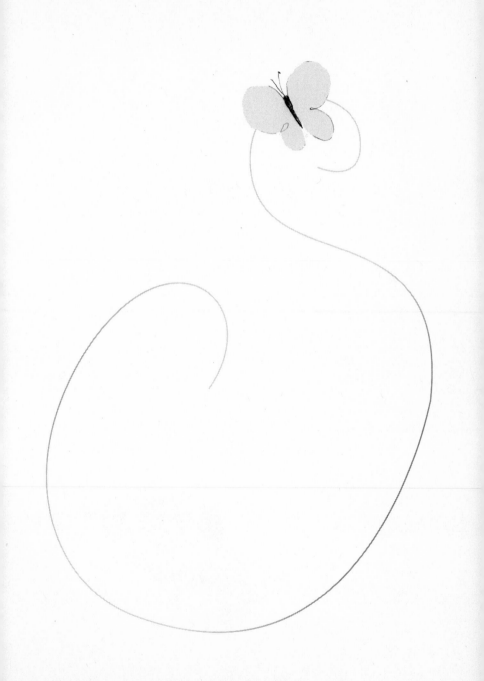

God grant me the senility

to forget the people I never liked anyway,

the good fortune to run into the ones I do,

and the eyesight to tell the difference.

ANONYMOUS

2
Retirement

Retirement has become a moveable feast in the Western world. Increased life expectancy and better health, combined with the escalating pension crisis, are pushing the boundaries. Some countries have already abolished a compulsory retirement age. Governments are actively encouraging their citizens to work well into their sixties and sometimes even into their seventies. And why not? Work can be a huge source of energy, creativity, and self-esteem. It provides income, intellectual stimulus, and challenge. It gives routine and structure to the week. How old is too old to work? "The days of our life are seventy years," says the Bible, "or perhaps eighty, if we are strong" (Psalm 90:10). With the advances of medical science even this is under review.

The new flexibility in the workplace is welcome because it means that the transition to our later years can be a relatively gentle affair. For those who can choose when to retire, retirement is no longer a threat. Many move first to working part-time, and then to working on an ad hoc basis before stopping altogether. The workplace remains attractive for a variety of reasons. Negatively, some still associate retirement with loneliness and boredom, and are determined to fend it off at all costs. Others, faced with the financial challenge of living longer on a fixed income, simply cannot afford to retire, or find themselves having to support not only their adult children but aged parents as well.

Failing health or stress can force some to seek early retirement. For them, it comes not a moment too soon, a blessed relief from commuting, from the pressure to perform and meet deadlines, or from having to maintain the fiction that everything is going swimmingly well. For those confronted with compulsory early retirement, there is neither choice nor flexibility. Being laid off can be a bitter blow, generating financial hardship and a collapse of self-esteem. Restructuring and downsizing are often euphemisms for disposing of those at the top end of the workforce. Finding a new job in your late fifties is a huge challenge. Suddenly you find yourself with time on your hands but less money in your pocket, and having to renegotiate your life.

Getting priorities right

Work may provide intellectual stimulation and routine, but it can also overwhelm and dominate. As Philip Larkin puts it in one of his poems, "Why should I let the toad work/Squat on my life?"[3] When priorities get distorted, relationships become strained and health suffers. In spite of our best intentions, it is easy to lose the plot and end up living to work instead of working to live. It is also possible to hide behind the demands of work to avoid difficult domestic situations. Work then becomes an excuse, or even an anesthetic, to blot out unhappiness. Some get sucked into a spiral of stress, driven by a frantic need to earn money to pay the mortgage, save for university fees, or look after frail parents.

None of us dare abdicate responsibility for the choices we make in middle age, including those about career and pension, lest we accelerate the journey "down Cemetery Road."[4] The number of men who die within two years of retirement is disturbing. This is often more complex than a simple reaction to the cumulative effect of stress during a working life. It can be in response to the shock of suddenly stopping or not adjusting psychologically to a new pattern of living. Some men just give up and die because they see no continuing purpose in staying alive.

As a young priest I took many funerals, among them of a man in his late fifties who died of a heart attack. I visited Jennifer, the widow, in preparation for the funeral. Sitting in their elegant home, surrounded by family photographs and holiday mementos, I listened to her desolation. Casting a hand around the room, she said, "Look at it all! I have all this stuff, but nothing I really want." Of course, what Jennifer wanted was the one thing she could not have, which was to have her husband back. But mingled with her grief was a regret at mistaken priorities. She admitted that in their preoccupation with buying a bigger and better house they had "lost sight of each other." So much of their life had been lived in the future, and that future never arrived.

We need to be alert to the danger of postponing our living until tomorrow or thinking that the only meaningful life is a busy one. When we are too busy we can easily lose a sense of proportion and end up discontented. We become trapped on a treadmill like pet hamsters, preoccupied with the acquisition of things or the longing for status. We fail to recognize the good things that we already enjoy, and when we attain what we are aiming for we do not get happier, we just want more. We never step back and ask ourselves what would be enough, because that would be the moment of realizing that nothing we could ever buy would bring happiness. If we do not grasp these important truths we will end up like Lady Macbeth: "Nought's had, all's spent, where our desire is got without content."

Animals have needs. Human beings have not only needs but also desires. Apparent wants can deceive. They are often temporary and superficial. Until we know what we really want and what we are seeking our lives will always be lived on the surface, and contentment will elude us. The feeling "there must be something more" will fill our waking hours. We slip into depression, and when we are depressed we become vulnerable to making bad decisions. Sometimes it is not until a crisis or bereavement overtakes us that we realize how unhappy we are or what we really want. When that wake-up call occurs, we should grasp it with both hands because it is full of potential.

Making the transition

How we make the transition into retirement depends not only on the priorities we have pursued, but also on how we see the future. Do we see retirement as a process of winding down? Or do we see it as being "given a new set of tires," being prepared for the next leg in life's journey?

In biology the term "irritability" refers to an organism's capacity to respond to external stimuli. An organism that exhibits no response is deemed dead. How we respond to the series of changes that retirement precipitates tests not only our maturity but also our liveliness. Resisting change can become a default option. Inertia is attractive because it makes few demands. Change and adjustment, on the other hand, although challenging and sometimes painful, at least provoke us into life.

Retirement is a step-change into a world that is both familiar and strange. "To make an end is to make a beginning. The end is where we start from," says Eliot in *Little Gidding*. He is right; but we should not underestimate the energy it takes to make an end. Sorting through files at the office, moving to a smaller house, saying goodbye to neighbors and colleagues, all take energy. Retirement is on a par with other changes in life: starting school, going to university, leaving home, finding a new job, getting married (or divorced), and parenthood. Transitions are not stress-free experiences. We need to be patient with ourselves and with our partners. It takes time to forge a different rhythm in life, and we need to adjust our expectations to match the new challenges confronting us.

Some people are only too happy to devote themselves to pruning the roses or attending watercolor classes. For them retirement presents no significant problems. But retirement can leave a person feeling acutely bereaved. You find yourself missing colleagues, even the ones you found irritating. You miss the network of relationships that was daily reality, and you pine for old watering holes. Part of your identity and sense of purpose in life has gone. You feel disoriented by the loss of structure and routine. And if you have moved house as well, you can be frustrated at how long it takes to settle and make new friends.

For all these reasons, retirement can precipitate a crash in confidence. You feel hesitant. Old certainties suddenly seem flimsy and it dawns on you that there are fewer years in which to discover new ones. You become oppressed by a sense of the clock ticking in the background and realize that you are not immortal after all. In all these experiences, naming the loss and recognizing what is going on can be profoundly helpful in adjusting to new realities.

Some find the transition to later life traumatic for different reasons. It is possible to deceive oneself for years and become adept at avoiding self-scrutiny. In fact the strategies adopted can be so successful that we end up not knowing what we feel about anything. Consciously or unconsciously, somewhere along the line we pressed the deep-freeze button. Now in retirement we find ourselves confronted with our unfinished business. We are forced to face questions that had been fermenting inside for years, and we panic lest we be overwhelmed by a tidal wave of unnamed doubts and fears, and not be able to cope.

The midlife crisis is well documented, though quite when midlife starts and ends these days is an open question. What is not well reported is the crisis that the transition to our later years can provoke. What may be relied upon is that if we do not deal with the issues that emerge in middle age, retirement will be experienced as threat, not opportunity. Questions can bubble up from the depths at any age, but they are guaranteed to come flooding to the surface when we have greater leisure and less energy to suppress them.

We should view these disturbances positively. They are opportunities for us to grow and be renewed so that we become more truly ourselves. Indeed it is possible to detect the hand of God in them. We regularly cast God in the role of comforter, but we forget that he may also be our dis-comforter, shaking us out of lethargy and disturbing our complacency.

Changing patterns of relationships

The most important things in life are not possessions but relationships, and in our Third Age we find them changing focus. Having dreaded the prospect of an empty diary, far from enjoying lazy mornings and putting our feet up, grandparents can find themselves thrust back into the role of parenting. Suddenly they are in demand to pick up grandchildren from school and operate a family taxi service. Newfound responsibilities can be fun and energizing, but may not be entirely welcome. Resisting pressure to run a free child-care facility is not easy. Working parents can expect too much of grandparents. They may have time, but they need to be asked what else they want to be and to do! As far as possible, all parties need to organize things so that grandparents' involvement with their grandchildren is a source of pleasure, not a burden.

Sometimes children are happier confiding in their grandparents than in their parents. Time is one of the gifts of retirement, and grandparents can choose to use it to foster a better quality of relationships across the generations. This can be uniquely rewarding. And, as friends often say to me, the wonderful thing about being a grandparent is that at the end of the day you hand the children back.

In contrast to the delight of grandchildren, what can be an unexpected and heavy burden is looking after elderly parents in their declining years. Frail and sometimes confused, they can be a major source of anxiety. Assuming power of attorney, arranging for additional home support, or negotiating a move into sheltered housing takes huge amounts of time and energy, and not a little sensitivity. For most of us, this is a natural expression of filial duty and love. But not everyone enjoys an easy relationship with their parents. When trust has broken down or there is an acrimonious family relationship, the offer of help can be spurned. Elderly parents may feel they are being patronized. How do we cope in such circumstances?

In the sixth commandment God does not require us to love our father and mother, but to honor them. Sometimes we cannot love one or both parents, and when this occurs it invariably induces terrible guilt feelings. God does not demand the impossible, but he does require that we honor those who gave us life. We need to release our parents from unrealistic expectations and respect them for who they are—fallible men and women who make mistakes like us.

Bizarrely, retirement can generate conflict between those who have been happily married for years. I recall one couple where the wife had a demanding job as the head teacher of a large comprehensive school. For years Sarah had come home to an empty house. During the hour or so before her husband returned from the office, she would putter round the silent house. Tired and "extraverted out" from school, she gradually unwound. However, following Graham's retirement, when she put the key in the lock she was greeted by a smiling husband eager to hear how her day had gone. What was offered as support was experienced as pressure. She retreated into herself, leaving him feeling hurt and confused. It took some time before they recognized the cause of the friction in their relationship. They negotiated a new pattern whereby Sarah would come home and Graham would give her space. They would rendezvous to watch the early evening news, and over a drink conversation would begin.

Retirement can sharpen our hold on life and make us determined not to fritter away our time on trivia. It directs our attention to things that really matter because it raises questions about self-worth and the quality of our relationships. The purpose of such questioning is not to demoralize us, but to provoke us into life. If we do not regain a sense of purpose in life, then it is highly likely that we will sink into lethargy. Jesus said that he had come that we "may have life, and have it abundantly" (John 10:10b). Abundant living is both God's promise and his gift. In our later years, no less than in our youth, we need to pray for grace to be open to it.

REFLECTION

How I choose to view retirement will color
how I envision the future. Am I retiring or being
"given a new set of tires" for the next leg of my
journey?

All transitions involve letting go and moving on.
Retirement, in particular, represents a series of
losses and gains. What have I lost and what have I
gained?

Retirement provokes questions about personal
integrity:

Am I making the best of my life?

What about the issues that I know I am not facing?

Am I living in a way that is in accord with my
conscience?

One should never count the years—one should count one's interests. I have kept young, trying never to lose my childhood sense of wonderment. I am glad I still have a vivid curiosity about the world I live in.

HELEN KELLER

3
Living

The late Queen Elizabeth the Queen Mother claimed never to have been bored. No doubt her privileged existence allowed her little time to be bored, though it is often the rich who are the most discontented. Boredom is the great disease of the Western world. It is no respecter of class or income, but the prospect of empty days filled with mindless repeats of third-rate television programs can haunt us as we contemplate the future.

Boredom is not a modern invention, but it is a prominent theme in many people's experience today. Even in a vibrant city like New York a graffito daubed on the wall of the subway could proclaim: "Tomorrow has been cancelled through lack of interest." Boredom is a strange amalgam of restlessness and dissatisfaction. It comes with a feeling of being stuck—in a dull job or a sterile marriage or in a part of town where nothing much happens. It is a symptom of feeling left out or left behind in a backwater while others are having fun or engaging in great enterprises.

Boredom is dangerous because it invites relief rather than cure. It tempts me to think that continuous activity and pleasure are the solution to my woes. It can generate a desperate, frenetic version of what it means to live life to the full. I end up compulsively busy and justify myself by my busyness. Pleasure alleviates boredom by distraction, but leaves the real me untouched. I can seek endless entertainment, but never liberate myself to live in a wholesome way.

If I am bored or frightened of becoming bored, then my first task is to unearth what lies underneath those feelings and look them in the face. How and why did they get there? This releases me from the power of buried feelings that hold me back. Boredom can be a symptom of a failure to accept myself. Whatever the diagnosis, I need to resist the fantasy of wanting to be someone else or to be somewhere else. I need to stick with me.

Getting the balance right

Maintaining a good work–life balance is a familiar mantra of self-help books. The advice is not new. It is the ancient wisdom of monastic spirituality. The timetable of a monastery is regulated to ensure that the first claim on a monk's energy is prayer and meditation. Each day is ordered to provide set periods for manual work, intellectual study, meals, domestic chores, rest, and relaxation. There are times for solitude and times in which the community comes together for recreation. St. Benedict insists that since body, mind, and spirit together make up the human person, all three deserve equal respect and should be catered for in the rhythm of the day. He values balance and moderation because they make possible an inner equilibrium that gently opens us to God. In Benedictine spirituality holiness and wholeness are two sides of the same coin.

In our latter years, free from the constraints of work and bringing up a family, we have a golden opportunity to re-order our week and achieve a more balanced and integrated way of living. For years we may have complained about not having time to pray or the energy to undertake projects. Those excuses have less validity in retirement when time is the one thing we do have. The challenge is to give energy to shaping an ordered, but less frenetic timetable in which our latent creativity can bear fruit. Our Third Age can be a time of rich fulfillment, an opportunity to achieve something worthwhile.

Being creative

We are not automatons. Made in the image of God and endowed with the divine spark of imagination, human beings are capable of immense creativity. Many people in their sixties and beyond are taken aback by the force of the urge within them to be creative. I remember one elderly nun who marked each decade of her life by learning something new. At the age of sixty Sister Jane Frances taught herself Spanish. At seventy she taught herself computing. By the time she was eighty she was confined to bed with osteoporosis of the spine. But this did not stop her putting the catalogue of the community library on disc, much to the amazement of her sisters. Sister Jane needed a way of expressing her inner vitality and her abiding desire to give.

By creativity, therefore, I do not necessarily mean being artistic or musical. I am referring to the whole gamut of human activity ranging from digging the back garden, fixing the car, making a home, cooking a meal for a friend, playing soccer with the grandchildren, writing poetry, to nurturing friendship. These things bring joy. Sometimes, of course, it is not lack of time or energy that is the problem. It is a fear of failure, of looking a fool, or a feeling that our creative gifts are too insignificant to bother with, that smothers our desire to "give it a go." If we succumb to these pressures we risk missing one of the joys of later life. There is no creativity without risk, and there is no risk without occasional failure.

When the wheels of my car were not properly aligned they had to be re-balanced lest I careered onto the sidewalk and killed someone. The mechanic told me that the car needed "geometry." The geometry of our wills needs similar treatment at the hands of God if we are to live in a wholesome way. Boredom is sterile and needs to be converted into the qualities that we see and admire in small children. Children are irrepressibly curious about life and full of questions.

Some time ago I met up with friends who have a four-year-old daughter. Ella had been playing happily in the garden as we drank coffee and chatted. Suddenly she came rushing in to tell us she had found some "crawlies" at the bottom of the garden. Pulling me up by the hand, she insisted that I come and look. For ten minutes or more we lay flat out on the ground and looked at a colony of ants as they marched to and fro in procession. Ella was captivated by the sight and totally absorbed. Which is why, to the amazement of his disciples, Jesus picked up a child, set it in their midst and announced, "Unless you change and become like children, you will never enter the kingdom of heaven" (Matthew 18:3).

Recovering a sense of wonder

As we grow older we have the opportunity to emulate young children and become re-enchanted with the wonder of life. God calls us into a more profound way of living that is both childlike and rich. In her novel *Middlemarch*, George Eliot puts into the mouth of her spirited heroine, Dorothea, a sentence that speaks of the beauty of life: "If we had a keen vision and feeling of all ordinary human life, it would be like hearing the grass grow and the squirrel's heart beat, and we should die of that roar which lies on the other side of silence." Eliot is telling us that we will cease to be bored the day we stop identifying "ordinary human life" with drabness and failure.

In a voyeuristic age of soap operas and lifestyle magazines, and where the Internet can be a distraction from the business of "real" life, it is tempting to live vicariously through others. The sight of the azure sea of the Mediterranean on television can blind us to the bright green grass of the local park. Pictures of an oceangoing yacht and its deep sofas can lead us to ignore the comfort we already enjoy. We become fascinated by the lives of celebrities and end up devaluing our own. We judge the worth of our lives by the perceived glamour of theirs and become embarrassed by our ordinariness. In short we become obsessed with what we do not have, and pass over the joy of family, the fun of having good friends, or the beauty of bare trees against a winter sky.

In moments of dissatisfaction and envy I need to ask myself, what would be enough? This is a contemporary version of the question the prophet Isaiah asked centuries ago: "Why do you spend your money for that which is not bread, and your labor for that which does not satisfy?" (Isaiah 55:2). It is easy to hold cheap what you see every day of your life. But if I lose interest in others I am in danger of devaluing the worth of my own life. If I become enthralled with fantasy I will miss the gift and miracle of each day.

Restlessness

We have more disposable income and greater leisure than at any other time in history, but many feel scared of having nothing to do. We are a restless generation, unable to settle. Writing in the late fourth century, Augustine prays, "Lord, you have made us for yourself, and our hearts are restless till they find their rest in you."[5] Augustine believes that God's gift of inner peace is available here and now. In his poem "The Pulley," George Herbert picks up Augustine's insight and explores it further:

> When God at first made man,
> Having a glass of blessings standing by;
> Let us (said he) pour on him all we can;
> Let the world's riches, which dispersed lie,
>   Contract into a span.
>
> So strength first made a way;
> Then beauty flow'd, then wisdom, honour,
>   pleasure:
> When almost all was out, God made a stay,
> Perceiving that alone of all his treasure,
>   Rest in the bottom lay.
>
> For if I should (said he)
> Bestow this jewel also on my creature,
> He would adore my gifts instead of me,
> And rest in Nature, not the God of Nature:
>   So both should losers be.

Yet let him keep the rest,

But keep them with repining restlessness:

Let him be rich and weary, that at least,

If goodness lead him not, yet weariness

May toss him to my breast.

What is magnificent about this poem is Herbert's certainty that God would find himself the loser if I do not turn to him. God wants me to be happy, to be at peace. For Herbert pleasure, beauty, friendship, all point beyond themselves to what is greater: God. What I need is located not in these wonderful things but beyond them. It is why I experience both ache and contentment. If meditating on the goodness of God fails to lead me to God, Herbert says, then exhaustion and dissatisfaction with the pleasures of life may yet succeed.

Leisure for God

The word "holiday," long before it was attached to seaside jaunts or exotic destinations, literally meant a "holy-day." It designated a festival or saint's day in the calendar of the church for which attendance at worship was obligatory. Life was punctuated by such commemorations and by the weekly observance of Sunday as a day of rest. The latter originated in the Jewish observance of the Sabbath, which Christians transferred to Sunday as a weekly celebration of Christ's resurrection. In combination this instilled a rhythm of work and prayer into daily life that shaped Christendom. It provided respite from drudgery and, in medieval times, an excuse for a bit of a party.

The deregulation of Sunday and the effective abandonment of trading restrictions have meant that this ancient rhythm has virtually disappeared, at least in Britain and North America. For some, the new flexibility is gain. For others, the fact that every day is now indistinguishable from any other day is loss. Those no longer in regular paid employment can be enveloped by a fog of sameness and find it difficult to establish a new routine.

In the Old Testament the word for holy, *qadosh*, is first applied not to a place or a person, but to time. "So God blessed the seventh day and hallowed it, because on it God rested from all the work that he had done in creation" (Genesis 2:3). Festivals are a feature of all religions, but there is something special about the Jewish Sabbath, with its emphasis upon rest from human effort. The Sabbath is not about the virtue of time management. It is a day of peace and quiet before God. It is not even about striving to find God. Instead I am summoned to rest with God and to share his Sabbath. It declares that I grow in wholeness and holiness by letting go and resting.

This insight is both intimidating and liberating. No matter our age, it invites us to forge a pattern of living in which work and creativity are complemented by rest and renewal. The point is not that if I am rested I will be more efficient and effective. The justification of leisure is not that I should function faultlessly without having a nervous breakdown, but that I should continue to be a human being. What is unique to Christian teaching is the belief that I become more myself as I rest in God.

Our culture grasps the point of leisure, but not the point of worship. We are happy to make time to go to the gym but not to pray. Prayer involves spending time with God, much in the same way that parents delight to be with their children. For prayer to be meaningful we need both to make time and to take time. Exercise, sports, music, painting, theater, cooking, gardening, playing bridge are all good things. But if we are to discover contentment as well as stimulus, we need to discover an equal leisure for God. We need to recover the dignity of both labor and leisure in life, and this is something older people can help society do.

Jesus says that unless we become as little children we shall never enter the kingdom of heaven. He says this not simply to encourage us to emulate a child's openness and trust, but because God waits to play with us for eternity. If we indulge our bored adult sophistication, we shall be bored for all eternity. Perhaps that is the ultimate definition of hell.

At a party I tried to offer an elderly lady a second glass of wine. "Don't worry about me," said Lotta, "I don't need the alcohol. I get sloshed on people." She had no time to be bored because she was interested in life and people, and delighted in them. She would have understood why it is that in the Bible the dominant image of heaven is not bored Botticelli angels playing harps, but a banquet, God's own party to which all are invited.

REFLECTION

Am I frightened of being bored? If so, why? What lurks underneath that fear?

The Third Age offers a host of new opportunities. If we are to make good choices, we need to ask ourselves some basic questions:

What am I really good at? What fires my creativity? What do I really want to do?

Go out for walk or sit in the garden. Take time just to be, to observe, to reflect. Pick up a stone or a flower and hold it in your hand. Take time to become re-enchanted with the wonder of life.

Review your daily or weekly pattern. Can you forge a better rhythm in which work and creativity are complemented by rest and renewal?

As you get older, three things happen.
The first is your memory goes, and I can't
remember the other two . . .

NORMAN WISDOM

4
Memories

An ability to remember the past and to envision the future distinguishes us from the rest of the animal kingdom. At school we cultivate our memory so that it provides the context and means by which we store and evaluate information. A sense of journey begins to emerge, of where we have come from and where we would like to be. The older we get, the more precious becomes the carpetbag of experiences we carry within us.

Memories infused with gratitude are the wonderful consolation of old age. We savor events that shaped us for good. But we can also find ourselves mourning opportunities we missed or mistakes we made. Augustine likens memory to a royal court full of people: some familiar, others strange; some delightful, others threatening and disturbing. "Inside me," he says, "is the huge court of memory in which I meet myself: I recall myself, what I have done, and how I was affected when I did it."[6] In our memories we do indeed meet ourselves: who we were and who we have become.

The story is told of the visit of a Member of Parliament to a residential care home in his constituency during the run-up to the General Election. Competing with the noise of the television, the politician uncharacteristically knelt down on one knee to speak to a resident. Full of self-importance, he asked the woman in a loud, somewhat patronizing voice, "Do-you-know-who-I-am?" The puzzled resident replied, "No, I don't. But if you go to reception, I'm sure you'll find someone who will tell you."

We retain personhood through our relationships. Memory is the matrix of our identity, which is why Alzheimer's disease is so terrifying. When memory fragments the self is lost. We no longer know who others are or who we are. As the wife of a former colleague said of her demented husband, "The lights are on, but there's no one at home."

Nurturing the corporate memory

Dementia not only affects individuals. It can also affect families, communities, and even nations. We saw it during the international banking crisis. The corporate memory of older bankers was squandered when they retired. A younger generation jettisoned their caution and thought they were invincible. They persuaded themselves that they could operate recklessly with impunity. Caught up in an economic fantasy, they fooled many into thinking that the unfettered (and virtually unregulated) market could go on delivering more and more wealth without anyone actually doing anything. They were wrong.

Without a memory society can lose its way.[7] Wisdom is lost in a morass of information.

Shameful episodes in a nation's or community's history are not confronted. Memories of embarrassment or humiliation are suppressed. Bereaved of the past, society becomes imprisoned in the present, vulnerable to the claims of expediency. In his novel *Nineteen Eighty-four*, George Orwell imagines a society in which the Ministry of Truth continuously edits newspapers to ensure that there is no memory of a time when Big Brother was not always right. Orwell realizes that when you control people's memories you control their capacity to imagine a different future.

What we remember, what we forget, and how we tell our stories, whether as individuals or communities or nations, are significant choices. If we are selective in what we remember we will end up being economical with the truth. Jesus famously said, "The truth will make you free" (John 8:32). The converse is equally true. The suppression of truth creates an illusion of peace, but never its reality. Selective amnesia distorts the past and promotes inaccurate or superficial remedies to problems. It shies away from dealing with underlying mistrust. Which is why the history curriculum and the integrity with which it is taught are ultimately moral issues. The memories of older people are powerful weapons in the fight against falsehood and tyranny.

Where is home?

Western society has become increasingly mobile. An unfettered market economy demands mobility. Better and cheaper transportation facilitates it. Increased immigration to service the needs of an ageing population has helped create a rich and diverse culture. But one casualty of this brave new world is a sense of belonging. As a generation, we have become rootless. We are no longer sure where home is or who we are.

The ancient Greeks had no trouble with belonging. They were proud of their city-states and readily identified with their place of birth. St.

Paul, sharing in the culture of the ancient world, tells us that he comes from Tarsus. He boasts of his Roman citizenship. He tells us that he is a Hebrew, born of the tribe of Benjamin, and a Pharisee by upbringing (Philippians 3:5). Paul had an instinctive sense of his place in the world.

Our medieval forebears' sense of belonging was shaped by the land they tilled and the parish in which they worshiped. Above all, they knew that at the end of their lives they would be buried in the churchyard alongside their relatives and neighbors. The community of the dead, through which they walked on their way to church on Sunday, fashioned a unique sense of belonging.

Some of these sensibilities were transferred from the villages to the new industrial towns of Britain, and in the Victorian era this was reinforced by a strong sense of civic pride. Well into the twentieth century families continued to live in close proximity to one another. Auntie might live round the corner; and grandparents, parents, and children might all live in the same house. A network of relationships provided care for elderly and children alike. But over the last forty years this has changed irrevocably. Family networks have come under strain and sometimes fragmented. Fewer people remain in the same job or town during their lifetime. And unlike earlier generations, many people do not know where they will die or be buried.

Small wonder that television series such as "Who do you think you are?" attract such huge audiences. People need to belong. They want to discover their roots. They are fascinated with plotting their family tree. On the day the national archives went on line the website crashed because of the huge interest from the public. In the search for identity the knowledge and memories of grandparents and older people are invaluable. They foster a renewed sense of belonging in their families and communities, not least because they alone know who's who in the photograph album.

The stories we tell

There is a connection between our identity as members of a family or community, and the stories we tell. It is by the things we remember and the way we remember them, and by the things we fail to remember, that we identify ourselves. It is why in the Bible the sharing of memories is a matter of religious obligation. In the Book of Deuteronomy, following the escape from Egypt, Moses instructs the people: "But take care and watch yourselves closely, so as neither to forget the things that your eyes have seen nor to let them slip from your mind all the days of your life; make them known to your children and your children's children" (Deuteronomy 4:9).

Sharing memories is an exercise of power. What we remember or choose not to remember shapes the present. It influences the behavior of others at a level deeper than conscious reflection. When our stories, with their instinctive emphases, distortions, and omissions are used to maintain grievance, to justify ourselves or put individuals in the wrong, we damage our family or community. Hatred can function like a virus. For a while it can go dormant, but it rarely dies. Instead it mutates, and we pass down our unresolved grievances to our children and to our children's children, who then feel compelled to defend our honor.[8]

I think of a family where the tension between father and son poisoned relationships. The conflict came to a head over a cousin's sixtieth birthday celebration. The son claimed that his father had said that he would never speak to him again if he went to the party. Geoff, the father, insisted that the real reason Jonathan had not gone to the party was because his daughter-in-law could not cope with their family. In the event not only did the son not go to his cousin's party, but also he wrote to his relations, blaming his father for his non-attendance. This caused a rift between Geoff and his brother's family, and between Geoff and his son, that to this day has not healed. Now in their late eighties, frail and isolated, Geoff and his wife are alienated from their family and feel powerless to effect any reconciliation.

Communities, like families, have long memories. Unaddressed grievances become part of the collective memory. When a perceived injustice is not addressed it gets written into the script that is then re-enacted at moments of crisis. Conflict and retaliation become inevitable. The seeds of vengeance germinate in the fertile soil of discontent. "It's all very well talking about burying the hatchet," a neighbor once said to me, "but you always know where you've buried it."

Healing painful memories

Who we are is what we remember, but memories can play tricks. I once listened while two friends, who were brother and sister, stumbled into an acrimonious conversation about their childhood. I wondered if it was the same family they were discussing, so irreconcilable seemed their versions of events. Eventually in an attempt to mediate, I suggested that they accept each other's experiences in good faith, recognizing that that is how it was for them and leave it at that.

Helen Bamber has worked extensively with survivors of the Holocaust and more recently with victims of torture. She knows the stuff of nightmares, but freely acknowledges memory's "ambiguity." In a conversation about her memories of Belsen concentration camp and how it has affected her to this day, her biographer records:

She talked about the camp's peculiar smell, and said that it was somehow the smell of geraniums. Not an unpleasant smell necessarily, but a sort of dank, sweetish odour that she cannot forget. She keeps geraniums on the patio of her small flat in London, and sometimes she is compelled to go out and smell them in their pots, for no reason that she can really articulate: the need to forget; the wish to remember.[9]

Many of us lodge painful memories. We desperately want to forget and move on. But at a deeper level we know that these experiences are such a fundamental part of our identity that we dare not let go of them. For the ancient Greek dramatist Aeschylus, memory distils raw experience into wisdom. It was the painful gift of the gods:

Even in our sleep
pain that cannot forget
falls drop by drop upon the human heart
until in our despair and against our will, there
comes wisdom
through the awful grace of God.[10]

In our memory we do indeed meet ourselves. And although these encounters at two o'clock in the morning when we cannot sleep are disturbing, they are ultimately healing. But healing is something we have to want. Evelyn Underhill,

one of the great mystical writers of the twentieth
century, recognized her ambivalence:

> O Lord, penetrate those murky corners
> where we hide memories and tendencies
> on which we do not care to look,
> but which we will not disinter
> and yield freely up to you,
> that you may purify and transmute them:
> the persistent buried grudge, the
> half-acknowledged enmity which
> is still smoldering;
> the bitterness of that loss
> we have not turned into sacrifice;
> the private comfort we cling to;
> the secret fear of failure which
> saps our initiative
> and is really inverted pride;
> the pessimism which is an insult to your joy, Lord;
> we bring all these to you,
> and we review them with shame and penitence
> in your steadfast light.[11]

Whenever we enter "the court of memory," we should do so in the awareness that we may harbor resentment without consciously knowing it. We need to pray, therefore, that God will disinter memories, however painful. This may stir up feelings of remorse, but remorse can unlock the future. It can enable us to come to terms with the past and attend to things we feel guilty about. We will never experience contentment if we are not at peace with our past. The goal of prayerful reflection is not the erasing of memories—this is neither possible nor desirable—but their healing.

Sharon was imprisoned for drug trafficking and assault, and her daughter taken into care. She registered on the prison's Narcotics Anonymous rehabilitation program. Entering upon Step 8, which required her to confront any whom she had hurt, she became terrified. Eventually her courage, fueled by a burning desire to be reunited with her daughter, enabled her to overcome her fear. "It blows me away," she said. "I don't want to do it, but I know I've got to." On the far side of a difficult series of meetings lay reunion with her daughter and the chance to build a better life together. Sharon wished to forget, but realized that she needed to remember, and that included saying sorry.

Without honest dialogue we will never know the extent of the damage we may have caused. And where there is no knowledge that a wrong has been committed, there will be no prospect of forgiveness that alone makes possible a different future. Some choose to conclude a false truce. Others suppress painful memories. They avoid talking about under-lying issues. They fear that an agenda might open up which could spin out of control and disturb the flimsy balance of a relationship. Even self-destructive situations can seem strangely comforting because they are predictable and familiar. If they lock into latent feelings of poor self-esteem, our inertia will become complete.

Remorse is painful, but it does make change pos-sible. It generates real conversations. Life is too short to postpone such encounters. Obviously we should be mindful of other people's sensitivities, but our aim should still be to "speak what we feel, not what we ought to say."[12] And for that we need both courage and humility.

REFLECTION

What can I contribute to the corporate memory of
my family/community?

Write down or record your memories of your life.
Sort out the family photographs and write on
the back who's who.

What do I want to be remembered for?

Nursing resentment is like eating poison
and waiting for the other person to keel over.

ANONYMOUS

5
Forgiveness

Close relationships draw out the best and the worst in us. All our relating is shot through with a degree of selfishness. The closer the relationship, the more likely this is to be the case. Even when we are deeply in love, our love will not be flawless. We put an extraordinary weight on relationships. We want the perfect lover or the ideal friend who can solve our problems, give us purpose in life, and be an object to whom we can be devoted. No human relationship can bear this strain.

One factor in the high level of marriage breakdown is the unrealistic expectations we harbor. We ask fragile human love to give us what only God can give. If I love in this way I am likely to turn the other person into an object that can be enjoyed, exploited, and if need be discarded. To love another person truly I must love them for who they are in themselves and not for what I can get out of them. I have to love them for their own good and not reduce them to the status of service provider.

Insecurity in relationships breeds either an unhealthy clinging to the other person, a longing to merge and get right inside them; or at the other extreme, a cool detachment, where I distance myself out of fear of intimacy. Mature relating is always a struggle. It helps when we address the causes of insecurity within us. We need to stay as separate persons relating to one another safely and sensitively. That includes maintaining respect for ourselves. If I cannot relate well to myself, I will not relate in a mature way to anyone else.

Unresolved conflict and guilt are two major causes of depression in later life. Painful episodes that we consigned to the cellar under lock and key finally catch up with us. The experience can be profoundly disturbing. Asked how they would like to die when the time comes, older people regularly say, "at peace and in my own bed"—at peace with others, at peace with themselves, and (if they are believers) at peace with God. They want in some indefinable way to hand back the gift of life with integrity. Facing the past, including our mistakes, is therefore too important a project to put off to our deathbeds. We need to get damaged relationships sorted now to the best of our ability and not leave things till it is too late. God does not demand that we get it right all the time, but he does ask that we acknowledge our faults and mistakes, and make amends.

Reconciliation

Acceptance and toleration are virtues in most circumstances, but they are insufficient to heal relationships that have gone seriously wrong, particularly in a marriage or family. The quick fix, the "kiss and make-up syndrome," will not work where feelings have been betrayed or humiliated. An apology is an important first step, but on its own it may not suffice. Ultimately only the offer and acceptance of forgiveness will secure healing. A passion for justice will move people a long way down the road to reconciliation, but only forgiveness will ensure that they are not destined to endlessly replay past grievances. Forgiveness gives us the ability to live with the past without being held captive by it. Forgiveness reshapes a family story and the way we tell it.

"Lord, how often shall my brother sin against me, and I forgive him? As many as seven times?" asks one of the disciples. Jesus replies, "I do not say to you seven times, but seventy times seven" (Matthew 18:22, RSV). The act of forgiving makes us bigger people. I take a step along this stony path every time I recognize my reluctance to let go of jealousy or hostility. It is so pleasant to hiss and grumble about how terrible someone else is because it takes the heat off me. Which is why I pray for the grace to want to forgive, and if need be, to desire to want to forgive. It is depressing how many seemingly impervious layers of hardheartedness the Holy Spirit has to percolate if my good intentions are to be anything more than that.

The problem about withholding forgiveness is that the person concerned is still making me suffer. By not forgiving we think that we are getting our own back. Better to be a victim than a loser, we say to ourselves. In reality, when we withhold forgiveness, we are the losers. When we forgive someone we let them go, and we ourselves are released from the events that have hurt and controlled us. They no longer have power over us. Which is why forgiveness is as important to the person who forgives as to the one who is forgiven.

Ray and Vi Donovan, speaking in a radio interview about the murder of their son in a random street attack, described their anger toward Christopher's attackers and how they screamed abuse at them. But the boy's mother also described how she gradually realized that her bitterness was destroying her. "It was like drinking a glass of poison and hoping it would poison them; only it did nothing." She went on to speak of her Christian faith and how she found the grace to forgive them, and how this has transformed her life. "Forgiveness has to be a choice," she said. In their case it was a choice that has led them to work with young offenders and, nine years beyond Christopher's murder, to become facilitators in a restorative justice program at a nearby prison.[13]

Reconciliation cannot always be effected overnight, and indeed may never be achieved. Forgiveness does not necessarily lead to reconciliation. We are talking about a process, not an event. If you break a leg, the limb has to be immobilized to allow healing to take place. Time and patience are essential. If this is true of broken bones, it is even more so with damaged relationships when trust has been fractured. Just because a wound is not visible does not mean that it does not exist. Hurt has to be understood, forgiven, and neutralized.

In 2007 the decision was taken not to deport Learco Chinadamo, the Italian juvenile killer of

Philip Lawrence. The head teacher had been stabbed to death protecting one of his pupils in a fight outside his school in 1995. Speaking on the radio about the Home Secretary's decision, Frances Lawrence, his widow, voiced her dismay. When questioned about her faith and the way this had "filtered" the experience and shaped her attitude toward her husband's murderer, she became confused. "Forgiveness," she said, "is a complex thing. I do not know what I am supposed to do. I have forgiven him intellectually, but viscerally— it's so difficult." When questioned further about her feelings she finally said, "I hope he makes something of his life." "Is not that a sort of forgiveness?" the interviewer asked. "I suppose it is," she replied.[14]

Forgiveness is indeed a complex thing. It takes time to permeate the different layers of mind and memory. Some dreadful things may lie beyond the capacity of humankind to forgive, at least in this life, and which only God can heal in eternity. The final exhibit in the Holocaust Gallery of the

Imperial War Museum in London is an audio-visual presentation. It consists of two large screens. The right-hand screen displays a succession of black-and-white pictures of the concentration camps as they appear today. Snow lends a veneer of beauty to derelict huts and barbed wire. But the railway line that led into Auschwitz, and the watchtowers, gas chambers, and crematoria, remain unmistakable.

The left-hand screen displays a series of interviews with Holocaust survivors, some of whom must have been children in the camps. The juxtaposition of the two screens, one silently showing black-and-white stills, the other animated and in color, is striking. The recollections of survivors do not make easy listening. "How wonderful that you should have forgiven them after all you've been through," says one woman. "Forgiven!" shouts her friend. "I can never forgive. How can you forgive what is unforgivable?" Some people's wounds go so deep that although they need to forget, they wish to remember. And who are we to condemn?

Forgive us as we forgive others

Enshrined at the heart of the Lord's Prayer is forgiveness. The prayer says that we cannot expect to be forgiven by God if we are not willing to forgive others. The Scottish translation of the prayer says, "forgive us our debts as we forgive our debtors."[15] The language of indebtedness highlights the damage that occurs when there is an imbalance of power, when one person or group has a hold over another. It inflates egos and encourages fantasies of power. Forgiveness sets individuals and communities on an equal footing. It restores self-respect.

When the Lord's Prayer was first translated in England during the sixteenth century, the phrase was rendered differently: "forgive us our trespasses as we forgive those who trespass against us." We do not use the word "trespass" much today apart from on notices declaring that "Trespassers will be prosecuted." Human relating includes a territorial dimension. Things go wrong when boundaries are not respected. We feel as though "our space has been invaded." In extreme cases a person can feel violated. Forgiveness in these situations will include the painstaking mending of broken fences, identifying and re-establishing boundaries so that trust may re-emerge. It is good to be open to others, but I must also protect my inner space. Only then will I be able to move in security and generosity toward others. This is particularly important in our later years when we can feel acutely vulnerable.

Forgiving ourselves

The final barrier to peace of mind is self-contempt. The forgiveness of God we can contemplate. Forgiving others (although vexatious) we can also contemplate. But forgiving oneself? Sometimes this

is a bridge too far. Self-contempt can hide beneath
a cloak of humility, and it needs to be unmasked.

"I'll never forgive myself for that," is a familiar
lament, and not just of the elderly. We can be
haunted by things we said in anger, people we
hurt or neglected, or the mistakes we made. All
of us rake over the past, often with good reason.
It is hard to let go of certain memories when
they keep springing up uninvited. But why can
we not find a way to let go of them? After all,
if God forgives us, why should we not forgive
ourselves?

Sometimes it helps to open up to a trusted
friend. Confession to a priest can also help. The
sacrament of reconciliation, as it is properly
called, enables us to be reconciled not only to one
another and to God, but to ourselves and our past.
It demands the abandonment of self-justification.
As we consciously and deliberately expose the
unresolved areas of our lives before God and seek
his forgiveness, God disinfects the hidden recesses
of our memories in which resentment breeds.

We cannot control the reactions of others. But we can choose what we say and how we say it. Good things are not done because we choose not to do them. Things are not said because we choose not to say them. Forgiveness is one of the choices that lies before us, and as the years pass its call becomes more urgent.

"I still can't quite believe the way it's all turned out," Margaret told me. "After working in the National Health Service all my life, I was dreading retirement. But amazingly, it feels as if everything in the first sixty years of my life has come together. I have discovered what it was all for. I've really got to know my godchildren, I've been going to French classes, and I've become a volunteer with the Citizens Advice Bureau. What seemed frightening is actually turning out to be rather wonderful." I was moved by her passion and energy. Here was someone who was grasping life with both hands and discovering new things about herself. For Margaret, retirement was not about shutting down, but about embarking upon a new phase of life.

Rediscovering who we are and making sense of
our life story is part of the adventure of growing
older. Without the constraints of employment, we
are free to be ourselves, even if that means con-
founding other people's expectations of us. New
horizons of exploration open up. Some choose to
assume responsibilities in the community, bringing to their new roles energy and the mature fruit
of experience. Others greet retirement with relief
and feel liberated. At last they can shed unwelcome
responsibilities.

REFLECTION

Are there things from the past where I am nursing grudges? How can I forgive and move on?

What can I do to bring about healing and reconciliation in my family where there has been breakdown?

If there is someone with whom I have unfinished business, why not write a letter or pick up the phone and sort it out?

What are the things that I need to let go of from the past—and where I do need to forgive myself?

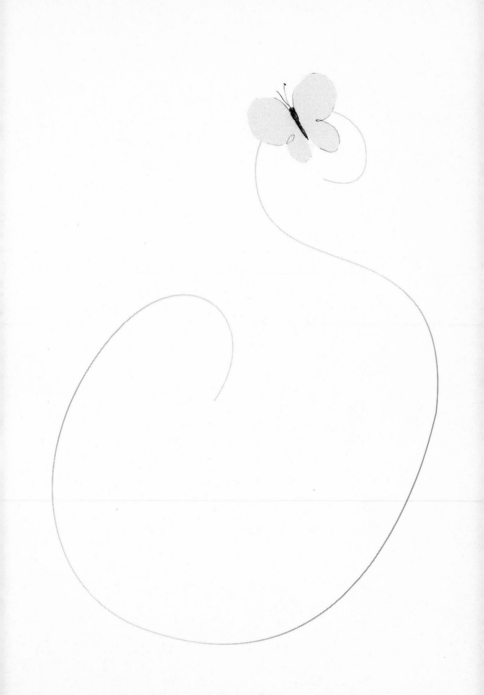

When I am an old woman, I shall wear purple

With a red hat that doesn't go, and doesn't suit me.

And I shall spend my pension on brandy and summer
gloves

And satin candles, and say we've no money for butter.

I shall sit down on the pavement when I am tired

And gobble up samples in shops and press alarm
bells

And run my stick along the public railings

And make up for the sobriety of my youth.

I shall go out in my slippers in the rain

And pick the flowers in other people's gardens

And learn to spit.

You can wear terrible shirts and grow more fat

And eat three pounds of sausages at a go

Or only bread and pickles for a week

And hoard pens and pencils and beer nuts and things
in boxes.

But now we must have clothes that keep us dry

And pay our rent and not swear in the street

And set a good example for the children.

We must have friends to dinner and read the papers.

But maybe I ought to practice a little now?

So people who know me are not too shocked and
    surprised

When suddenly I am old, and start to wear purple.

JENNY JOSEPH

6
Becoming

Retirement is a mixed bag. The changes it brings are both exciting and unsettling. One minute you feel energized by a new opportunity. The next you are plagued by self-doubt. Former colleagues promise to keep in touch but forget, and you find yourself unwittingly reassessing the worth of your career. The children, who had occupied such a central part of daily existence, have fled the nest. Suddenly the family home feels oppressive, silent, and empty. Visions of happy days taking grand-children to a soccer game or to Peter Pan fail to materialize. Retirement may be the first time for years that a couple has spent any significant time in each other's company, and unexpectedly they find themselves having to get to know each other again. Who is this person sitting opposite me at break-fast? Even more urgent, who am I without my role as parent and homemaker, or without the affirmation that my job gave me?

We all want to be fulfilled and to make something of our lives. When we are young broadening vistas excite us. We take risks. Ambition drives us forward. The adrenaline flows. This is natural and good, but ambition can become distorted and lead us to act callously. We become vulnerable to ugly qualities like ruthlessness, greed, and disloyalty. If self-assertion becomes our instinctive way of self-expression, then it is likely that we will sacrifice friends and family on the altar of personal realization with the result that when retirement arrives, so does loneliness. The years go by and we realize with increasing clarity that not everything is possible after all. "Time running out now and the soul unfinished,/And the heart knows this is not the portrait it posed for," laments R. S. Thomas in his poem *Self-Portrait*.[16]

Mercifully, the negative effects of ambition are often counterbalanced, or at least mitigated, by those around us. Having children and raising a family are joys of life, bringing a deep sense of fulfillment. A family knows our strengths and weaknesses. They can tell us the truth about ourselves. At its best, therefore, family life is profoundly converting, knocking the ego off its perch and forcing us to take account of others and be less selfish. The happiness of others matters. Unfortunately, if we have become self-obsessed, the force of this simple but profound truth may not dawn on us until it is too late. Self-scrutiny is vital, and it needs to be matched with respect and sensitivity to others. Without it we are liable to damage the people we love.

Self-knowledge

Gregory of Nyssa, writing in the fourth century, says that self- knowledge is our greatest protection in life: "How can you protect a person you do not know? Each of us must know ourselves as we are, and learn to distinguish ourselves from what we are not. Otherwise we may end up unconsciously protecting somebody who does not exist, and leave our true selves unguarded."[17] Gregory's advice should be set alongside Jesus's statement that "when the Spirit of truth comes, he will guide you into all the truth" (John 16:13). One old monk told me this is the most terrifying verse in the Bible. Lies enslave, he used to say, and the worst lies are the ones we tell ourselves.

In *The Lord of the Rings* the Ring Wraiths, mounted on horses and swathed in black cloaks, appear out of swirling darkness like the Horsemen of the Apocalypse. They are terrifying because there is nothing beneath their hoods. They are creatures without faces. If I collude with self-deceit and tell lies to myself, I am in danger of losing all sense of my true self. I may wear now one mask and now another, and never appear with my true face. But choices have consequences. If I lie to myself and to others, I cannot expect to find truth and reality whenever I happen to want them. If I choose to live a lie I should not be surprised that truth eludes me when I most need it.

We are all chameleons. Different people see different aspects of our personalities. Few see us whole. We need to cultivate a strong sense of ourselves to carry us through the years ahead. Self-knowledge helps us to handle other people's perceptions of us. Older people can be particularly vulnerable in this respect. As one feisty ninety-year-old said to me, "The trouble about being in a wheelchair is that people no longer treat you as an adult. They either talk over your head or talk down to you. I may not be able to walk, but I'm not daft." The interest and attention we receive from others matters. I remember speaking to an elderly resident in a care home about his insomnia. Dennis told me that he whiled away the long hours of the night by reading. "What do you read?" I inquired casually, anticipating a banal reply. "Proust, mainly," he said. I was duly cut down to size. Older people are indeed full of surprises.

Some people are self-assured and never worry what others think of them. The majority of us are less resilient. If people laugh at my jokes I become confident in my ability to amuse. On the other hand, if they avoid me in the street or appear bored by my anecdotes I easily fall prey to self-doubt. In an ideal world it should not matter two hoots whether or not someone remembers my name, or if a neighbor cuts me dead. As it is, I fret when these things happen, and I find myself going over the episode until it eventually loses its power over me. I have yet to learn to let go of the petty rivalries and insecurities that plague me, and grow in self-acceptance and generosity to others.

Sadly, we all know of individuals where, in old age, disease and chemical changes to the brain have effected irreversible changes in their personality. But I have also seen how a person's true character can emerge in later years. I remember two elderly solicitors. One was the quintessential English gentleman: polite, cultivated, and punctilious. The other was shy, well defended, and remote. In their last years I watched the first become increasingly embittered and demanding.

It became clear that beneath his cultivated exterior lurked a sad, rather self-centered person. Whereas behind the unsmiling face of the other solicitor was a gentle person trying to get out. As he aged he relaxed, and a man of quiet serenity emerged. He was a good listener, and I was not the only one who enjoyed his company. In old age neither man had the energy to maintain the masks with which they had habitually disguised their true selves from the world. The masks slipped, and their true character emerged for all to behold.

The real me

Rabbi Meshulam Zusya of Hanipoli, the great Hassidic leader and scholar of Eastern European Jewry of the eighteenth century, encouraged his congregation to stop comparing themselves with other people who may seem more attractive, more intelligent, more gifted or just nicer. "In the coming world," he used to say, "they will ask me not, 'Why were you not the great Abraham or Moses?' but 'Why were you not Zusya?'" We should stop trying to be somebody else. We should concentrate on being whoever we are, confident in God's love for us. In retirement we have the best chance in our lives to do this. With less to prove and less to lose we can dare to be ourselves. As Jenny Joseph remarks in her poem about growing older, "When I am an old woman I shall wear purple, with a red hat that doesn't go." But this takes courage.

Whether or not we sport purple clothes, sit down on the curb when we are tired, or run our walking stick along the railings, being true to our-selves, being the "real me," far from alienating us from God, draws us closer. God invites us to work with him in the creation of our identity. He leaves us free to be ourselves, or not. We are at liberty to be real or unreal, true or false. We should not kid ourselves that this can wait and let matters ride. There are real choices to be made. I know that unless I actively decide to work with God in

this extraordinary enterprise it will never happen.
I also know what will be the end product of my
failure to cooperate: I will end up Mr. Grumpy.

Searching for God

The quest for self-knowledge is universal and
lifelong. Even the apostle Paul observed, "I do not
understand my own actions. For I do not do what I
want, but I do the very thing I hate" (Romans 7:15).
Frustration, lack of self-control, powerlessness, and
a longing for self-understanding are things we all
experience. In the Christian tradition, however,
self-exploration is subsumed and shaped by a more
profound quest: the search for God. It is not who
we are, but who God is that is all-important. If old
men ought to be explorers, then this is the ultimate
challenge. What does the Bible say?

At first glance it is disappointing because it
appears to answer few of the questions we want

answered about life, the world and the universe. Not
unreasonably, we assume that this is great literature
about the quest for personal enlightenment. In
the opening pages of Genesis, however, it is not
man's search for God that is described, but God's
search for us. The first question is not, "Where are
you, God?" but "Where are you, Adam?" And this
is followed by three more questions: "Who told
you that you were naked?" "What is this that you
have done?" and "Where is your brother?" (the last
being in response to the murder of Abel by Cain).
Opportunity, sin, shame, guilt, lies, envy, murder are
all here. Spiritual awakening begins when we hear
these divine questions addressed to us personally. It
is as we wrestle with these questions that the search
for God and the search for self come together.

Becoming the unique person God has it in mind
for me to be is a lifetime's journey. As Paul says,
"For now we see in a mirror, dimly, but then we
will see face to face. Now I know only in part; then
I will know fully, even as I have been fully known
(1 Corinthians 13:12). Augustine believed that the

search for God and the search for self are two sides of the same coin because we are made in the image of God. "If I knew myself," he argued, "I would know God."[18] He says that the deepest truth about our nature is that in God we discover who we really are. This is why we should focus our energy not in seeking happiness or self-fulfillment or even self-knowledge, but in seeking God.

God is both familiar and strange, beyond us and yet strangely within. God is not an object to be observed, or a pet to be tamed and discarded at whim. God is an inexpressible, fascinating, transcendent mystery who invites us into loving intimacy. Which may be why prayer to this *incognito* God, at least in my experience, is such a hit-and-miss affair. Many of the great spiritual writers share their frustration with this elusive "hide and seek" God and testify to the ambiguity of their religious experience. One moment prayer is fresh and energizing, the next moment arid and sterile, leaving you perplexed. It is as if God is always one step ahead, as if he has just left the room as you

enter it. We sense his presence and feel compelled
to follow. In the words of the poet R. S. Thomas:

> He is such a fast
> God, always before us and
> Leaving as we arrive.[19]

In Christian thought our longing for God is
a response to the God who is searching for us,
although it may not always feel like this.

When I pray I am sharing in a conversation that
God has started. The New Testament speaks of
the divine initiative in these words: "In this is love,
not that we loved God but that God loved us and
sent his only Son to be the atoning sacrifice for
our sins" (1 John 4:10). St. John is articulating the
central claim of the Christian faith: the unseen
God has made himself known in the Crucified
One. In Jesus I encounter not only the human face
of God but also the contours of my own face. In
Christ I finally become who I am.

REFLECTION

Spend some time reflecting upon the four great questions of Genesis:

"Where are you?" Where am I at this point in my life?

"Who told you that you were naked?" Are there things of which I am ashamed?

"What is this that you have done?" Are there areas in my life where I have not taken responsibility?

"Where is your brother/sister?" What responsibility do I have toward my family, friends, and neighbors? What can I do to make a difference?

Teach us so to number our days that we may apply our hearts unto wisdom.

PSALM 90:12
Book of Common Prayer

7
Happiness

Traveling on a packed London underground train, I watched a young man engrossed in his book. As he left the train I caught sight of the title: *Instant Confidence: How to go for everything you want*. Getting what I want and getting it now is a popular solution to life's problems. As a generation we crave immediate satisfaction and dislike waiting. Only there are no short cuts to happiness. When human aspiration is cheapened we end up discontented. Happiness is not something we can buy along with a new television.

Identifying what we truly want is important, but it may take time to discern our deepest hopes and longings. As I grow older I am becoming more realistic in my expectations. Life is not as straightforward as I once thought. Part of growing in maturity is realizing I cannot have everything my own way. Coming to terms with this will contribute to whether I enjoy a sense of contentment in my latter years or end up sour and resentful. Contentment should be the crowning glory of our lives, but it is often notable by its absence.

Resentment is more than disappointment. It has a hard, bitter edge fueled by jealousy of other people's good fortune—and recrimination at the catalogue of our failures. Unlike anxiety, which can gnaw away undetected, anger and resentment are easier to identify. I know when I am angry with someone. I then have the choice to give in to it, or to rise above it and free myself from its poison.

Contentment emerges as we face our demons and integrate our disappointments. It is the fruit of the way we live, including a positive attitude toward other people's good fortune. Søren Kierkegaard says that self-absorption is the enemy of contentment because "the door to happiness always opens outward."[20] Above all, a contented life is one characterized by thanksgiving for what we have rather than moaning about what we do not have, or what advertisements tell us we ought to have.

Gratitude

For those fortunate enough to have had a productive and fulfilling career or a happy family life, the idea of giving something back to others makes sense. When we acknowledge life as a gift and not a possession, we become less self-centered and more willing to share the good things of this world with others. Gratitude enriches. It generates an inner freedom that turns duty into joyful service.

Happiness is not something we can achieve, like getting a promotion or passing our driving test. It creeps up unannounced as a by-product of the way we live. William Law, an eighteenth-century spiritual writer, says that giving praise to God is "the surest way to all happiness and perfection. . . .

Whatever calamity happens to you, if you thank and praise God for it, it turns into a blessing. Could you therefore work miracles, you could not do more for yourself than by this thankful spirit. It turns all that it touches into happiness."[21]

The circumstances of our lives may or may not be open to the possibility of change. What is open to change is how we choose to view a situation, including the past and the decisions we made when we were younger. Seeing things in a new light, though it may require the grace of God and not just an act of will, can liberate us from cycles of self-recrimination. Giving thanks to God unlocks the imagination and enables us to move on—to live now. For W. H. Auden, it is the praise of God that irrigates "the deserts of the heart" and brings healing:

> In the deserts of the heart,
> Let the healing fountain start.
> In the prison of his days,
> Teach the free man how to praise.[22]

Joy

What are the roots of joy in our life? Jesus promises his disciples that his joy would be in them and that no one would be able to rob them of it. In the New Testament joy is one of the fruits of the Spirit, the product of faithful discipleship and openness to the leading of God's Spirit. St. Paul says that it goes hand in hand with love, peace, patience, kindness, generosity, faithfulness, gentleness, and self-control (Galatians 5:22). We should not expect its presence, therefore, in isolation from other virtues. Our task is to cultivate "the deserts of the heart" so that in old age it bears a rich harvest. Interestingly, the word *happiness*—so common in our culture—does not feature in Paul's list.

In English the word "happiness" is related to "happen." Both words have a common root in the Middle English "hap," meaning chance or fortune. From this root a range of vocabulary has developed for the way life pans out, either for good or for bad. There is the term "mishap" for a bad occurrence, and "haphazard" meaning randomly. Happiness describes a state of mind shaped by what "happens," which presumably is why we make an effort to control events and minimize risk. This may be sensible, but it would be foolish to think that if only we could get the circumstances of our lives right, then we would be happy. In my experience happiness is more a matter of direction, choice, and habit, and less an accident of circumstances. We need to be alert to the twin dangers of postponing living until things (we hope) are better, or opting out of the present into the past. The older I get, the more powerful the latter temptation becomes.

The providence of God

Francis de Sales, writing in the sixteenth century, links contentment to the providential care of God. He sees it as God's supreme gift. He compares our relationship with God to that of a child going out for a walk. He pictures a child strolling along a country lane, hanging on to his or her parent with one hand, while happily picking blackberries and wild strawberries with the other. And that is how it should be, says Francis. God wants us to delight in the world. But, he warns, we should be careful not to get distracted or greedy, and attempt to accumulate too many things on our journey through life. If we let go of God's hand in order to pick more and more strawberries we will end up flat on our face:

Throughout your life, learn to trust in the providential care of God, through which alone comes contentment. Work hard, but always to cooperate with God's good designs. Let me assure you, if you trust all to God, whatever happens will be the best for you, whether at the time it seems good or bad to your own judgment. . . . God will work with you and in you and for you throughout your life. And at the last you will know that you have not labored in vain, and be filled with a profound contentment that only God can give.[23]

Francis de Sales's teaching on trust echoes that of Paul: "I have learned to be content with whatever I have. I know what it is to have little, and I know what it is to have plenty. In any and all circumstances I have learned the secret of being well-fed and of going hungry, of having plenty and of being in need. I can do all things through him who strengthens me." (Philippians 4:11–13)

The word that St. Paul uses for contentment was well-known in Greek ethics. It meant "being entirely self-sufficient." Contentment was a favorite virtue of the Cynics and Stoic philosophers.[24] They argued that you achieved contentment by being independent of everything and everyone. In order to secure invulnerability they advocated the elimination of all desire. The Stoics rightly believed that contentment does not consist in possessing much but in wanting little. However, they proposed systematically getting rid of every emotion until you achieve an inner disposition of no longer needing or caring what happens to you or to anyone else. This involves the abolition of desire and the eradication of emotion. The Stoics made the heart a desert and called it peace. They believed that nothing can happen that is not the will of God. However painful something might be they believed it must be God's will. Contentment is achieved by a deliberate decision to see in everything—however disastrous—the will of God.

Stoicism still appeals to those who subscribe to the British philosophy of the stiff upper lip, but it is inimical to the spirit of the gospel. Christianity does not preach fatalism. Not everything is sent

by God. Christians distinguish what God permits
from what he purposes. God's good purposes will
not be frustrated by human sinfulness, but for
the sake of our freedom he permits certain ills.
Christian spirituality is about the expansion of the
human heart, not its contraction. It is about the
purification of our desires, not their suppression.
For Paul contentment is not an act of will, but a
gift of God: "I can do all things through Christ
who gives me strength." The Stoics boasted of
their self-sufficiency. Paul, hijacking their language, boasted of the God who met his needs.
And it is this understanding that should inform
our prayer.

The prayer of protest

"The trouble with you Christians is that you are
far too polite to God," a rabbi once said to me. Jews
are less deferential to the Almighty than Christians.

As the psalms testify, Jews are neither ashamed nor afraid to express raw emotion before God. Christians tend to edit their feelings, particularly anger. Some editions of the psalms suggest that verses expressing anger and violence should not be used in public worship lest they offend liberal sensibilities. But if we edit out the angry bits, why not also the smug bits?

The psalms need to be prayed, not sanitized. They offer a rich vocabulary with which to pray. They give us permission to protest injustice, to be angry in the face of cruelty, to lament the death of friends, to be who we are before God. "So even to old age and gray hairs, O God, do not forsake me, until I proclaim your might to all the generations to come" (Psalm 71:18). Contentment is not resignation in the face of life's tragedies. It is the fruit of the struggle to act and pray honestly. We need to pray as we are, not as we would like to be. It takes time and effort to be elegant in prayer, but only honesty to be real. God wants our prayer real rather than elegant.

At the end of the American Civil War, in the diary of an unknown Confederate soldier, was discovered this entry:

I asked God for strength that I might achieve.

I was made weak that I might learn humility.

I asked for health that I might do greater things.

I was given infirmity that I might do better things.

I asked for riches that I might be happy.

I was given poverty that I might be wise.

I asked for power that I might have the praise of men.

I was given weakness that I might feel the need of God.

I asked for all things that I might enjoy life.

I was given life that I might enjoy all things.

I got nothing I asked for,

but everything I hoped for.

Almost despite myself,

my unspoken prayers were answered;

I am, among all men, most richly blessed.

The soldier had learned that prayer is not about coercing God but being in communion with him. He discovered that, although God may not have given him everything he had asked for, he had given him everything he genuinely needed, and as a result he felt blessed.

Sally was in her late forties when she was diagnosed with Alzheimer's. The disintegration of her personality from a bright, vivacious person to a confused, prematurely old woman was terrible. Her diminishment was protracted and inexorable. At the end she lay in a cot with round-the-clock nursing. I do not know how her husband coped or what he prayed, but I do know that each day he would come home and chat to her as if nothing had changed, exchanging family news and gossip, smoothing her hair, holding her hand. Their relationship became more intimate through this terrible suffering, and it enriched all who knew them. It is in the opaqueness of such experiences, which both deny and affirm the goodness of God, that the concept of being blessed by God becomes flesh, honoring the contradictions of life without attempting to resolve them.

The eighteenth-century Jesuit Jean-Pierre de Caussade in his letters of spiritual direction urges us to bring the whole of our life into our prayer, including those things that appear to contradict God's purposes of love. Faith, he says, is like a scalpel that dissects painful experiences. It "cuts through these appearances, grasping the hand of God who keeps us alive."[25] Such surgery of the soul is energized by the conviction that somehow God is to be discovered in the mess and pain holding out his own wounded hand. It was de Caussade who coined the phrase "the sacrament of the present moment" to describe how the will of God can be embraced in every moment of every day.

If we treat every encounter as an opportunity in which to meet God, and if we actively seek his will, then we will find him. With the eye of faith, we can meet Christ not only in our friends and family, but also in the faces of strangers and enemies.

Every moment can become a sacrament and every meeting an encounter of grace.

In my life there have been moments when the sight of a sunset or the sound of a child practicing the piano through an open window has inexplicably moved me and I have felt close to God. Equally there have been occasions of pain and dereliction when I have become aware of the presence of God. Like Jacob, who wrestled with a stranger beside the ford of the Jabbok all night (Genesis 32:24–32), I have felt more alive, not less so. All of which leads me to the realization that God is always with me. Happiness may come, happiness may go, but God abides. Here is the root of joy and the foundation of a contented life.

REFLECTION

What are the roots of joy in my life?
What are the things that bring me contentment?
Make a list and spend five minutes each day giving
thanks for them.

How can I live in the present moment more fully,
and allow it to become a sacrament?

It's only when we truly know and understand that we have a limited time on earth . . . and that we have no way of knowing when our time is up . . . that we will begin to live each day to the full, as if it were the only one we had.

ELIZABETH KÜBLER-ROSS

8
Finale

In 1961 Dag Hammarskjöld, the Swedish statesman and Secretary General of the United Nations, was killed in a plane crash. Following his death, his journal of reflections was published under the title *Markings*. Among his observations one entry proved inspirational to many older people: "Night is drawing nigh. For all that has been—thanks! To all that shall be—Yes!" There can be few better mottos to accompany us during our later years.

The feeling that we have not lived life to the full can undermine a sense of well being. But if this is the case, as we contemplate the future, our goal should not be to do more, but to be complete. Self-knowledge, prayerful reflection, savoring happy memories, thanksgiving for what has been, and openness to what shall be all contribute to our contentment. They help us to be at peace with ourselves and with other people. Quantity of years does not necessarily equate to quality of life.

As we pass the four score years' milestone we can find ourselves confronting a unique set of challenges: increasing frailty, memory problems, hearing loss, failing health, and decreasing mobility. If the challenge of the middle-aged is to deal with the fear of failure, as we enter our final years it is learning to handle the fear of weakness. Health creates a freedom we rarely notice until we no longer have it. Not being able to do simple things is frustrating. As my eighty-eight-year-old father said to me, "It's tough growing old." Retaining a sense of well-being when your week is dominated by trips to the hospital or you are dependent on others for the necessities of life is difficult.

Coping with loss

If we are to discover at the end of our days that life is still worth living, then we have to know that we ourselves are worthwhile. Loneliness is a big problem, particularly in our cities with their anonymous streets and transitory populations. Older people easily become isolated. Remaining connected is a daily challenge. Rarely being physically touched can contribute to a sense of isolation. We all need affection, to be loved and affirmed. We give affection readily to children, but can forget to give it to older people. However, in the autumn of life we need it just as much as when we were young.

One group of elderly and mainly housebound ladies has refused to surrender. Unable to be of practical service any longer, they have formed themselves into an "emergency prayer network," determined to radiate God's love to those around them. Those in need of prayer phone Doris, the convener, who alerts the next in the chain and so on. Not only does their concern generate a wave of supportive prayer across the community but, by their own admission, putting others at the center of their attention prevents them from becoming self-preoccupied. It keeps them in touch and breaks down a sense of isolation. Being the generation they are, they are also good at writing letters. In an age of e-mails, receiving a personal handwritten letter is an unusual event for many young people. Quite by accident, these old ladies have found a way of expressing their care across the generation gap, and it is warmly appreciated.

For most of us the biggest challenge by far in our later years is maintaining confidence and self-esteem in the face of the loss of independence.[26] Giving up your car and stopping driving is a watershed that most face at some point. Many delay making the decision out of fear of isolation. They sense it to be the thin edge of the wedge. For a minority, increasing frailty precipitates a move into sheltered housing. This can come as a relief, but it can be traumatic when it includes not only giving up your home, but moving to another part of the country in order to be near a son or daughter. This may make admirable sense to the rest of the family, but the loss not only of home, but the network of neighbors and friends as well can be distressing. Living in a residential community of people you have not chosen can be a bitter pill to swallow. Company is not the same thing as companionship.

If Dag Hammarskjöld provides a motto for later years, perhaps the words of the Risen Christ to Peter provide the text. "When you were younger, you used to fasten your own belt and go wherever you wished. But when you grow old, you will stretch out your hands, and someone else will fasten a belt around you and take you where you do not wish to go" (John 21:18). How do we pray in these circumstances?

Prayer and contemplation

Being present to God as we are is the basis of all prayer. In our later years the prayer of reminiscence may become a regular way of praying. We find ourselves looking back on our life and savoring our memories. We give thanks to God for good times. But reminiscence can equally lead to sadness, puzzlement, and regret. These too should feed our prayer. We may find it difficult to sustain concentration, but the intention to pray is more important than attention in prayer.

Prayer is likely to be a simpler affair than when we were young, less intense and more contemplative. Allowing God to pray in us, receiving his love and affirmation, can be life-sustaining when energy levels are low. "Be still, and know that I am God!" (Psalm 46:10) is a great text for prayer whatever our age and situation. When this psalm was translated into Latin, the Hebrew was rendered slightly differently: "Empty yourself and know that I am God."[27] We need not only to be still, but also to empty ourselves of cynicism and bitterness to allow God access to our heart.

This surrendering of the will is something Christian mystics talk about. They describe it not as the cancellation of the self, as if God had won a victory over us, but a process by which we rest in God. Sometimes God can seem remote or even absent. More often than not it is we who are the absentee. We are not sufficiently at home in our bodies to receive him. True prayer, therefore, is rooted in being ourselves in the assurance that God understands and loves us. Through prayer we learn to inhabit our life more fully.

Immanuel Kant, the great German philosopher, said that there are only three questions in life worth spending time on: What can I know? What ought I to do? And what may I hope? It is the third question that comes to the fore as we go into extra time. What is there to look forward to?

The last lap

"I go to so many funerals these days," an elderly neighbor once said to me, "and they're all my friends." The inevitability but unpredictability of death hovers in the background, and not always just in the background. It has been my privilege to be with a number of people as they died. Some were frightened not of annihilation, but of absurdity. Death sealed for them the emptiness of a life not fully lived. Death came too soon, before they could make sense of their life, before they could make one last attempt to give it meaning. Some of them became vulnerable to attacks of despair in which their sense of the value of all that had gone before them drained away. The sting of death was not the loss of life, but the loss of meaning.

Bronnie West, an Australian nurse specializing in palliative care, questioned her patients about any regrets they had or anything they would have done differently.[28] Five themes surfaced again and again.

1. "I wish I'd had the courage to live a life true to myself, not the life others expected of me."

2. "I wish I hadn't worked so hard." This was a frequent regret of her male patients, many of whom felt they had missed their children growing up because they had been preoccupied with their work.

3. "I wish I'd had the courage to express my feelings." Many people had suppressed their feelings in order to keep the peace with others, and ended up embittered.

4. "I wish I had stayed in touch with my friends." There were deep regrets about not having given friends the time and effort they deserved. Some had let friendships slip.

5. "I wish I'd let myself been happier." Many did not realize till the end of their lives that

happiness is a choice. They had opted for the comfort of familiarity, fearing change, and settled for a mediocre existence.

Bronnie West's findings tally with several of the themes explored in this book. But she also records that, faced with their mortality, people often change and can grow enormously.

Death has always evoked a variety of responses ranging from denial, anger, defiance, recognition, and fear, to calm acceptance. With less of life to look forward to, the past comes into sharp relief. Some, with the poet Dylan Thomas, want to rebel against its encroachment:

> Do not go gentle into that good night,
> Old age should burn and rave at close of day;
> Rage, rage against the dying of the light.[29]

There is a time and a place for anger, but there is also a time and a place to go gentle into God's good night.

Thinking about death does not have to be a grisly, morbid affair. French philosopher Teilhard de Chardin found it sharpened his hold of life and deepened his desire for God. He saw old age, illness, and even mental confusion as opportunities to prepare him for the biggest adventure of all— the final surrender into the arms of God in death:

When the signs of age begin to mark my body (and still more when they touch my mind); when the illness that is to diminish me or carry me off strikes from without or is born within me; when the painful moment comes in which I suddenly awaken to the fact I am losing hold of myself and am absolutely passive within the hands of the great unknown forces that have formed me; in all those dark moments, O God, grant that I may understand that it is you (provided only my faith is strong enough) who are painfully parting the fibres of my being in order to penetrate to the very marrow of my substance and bear me away within yourself. . . . Teach me to treat my death as an act of communion.[30]

God of our journey

People often talk about life as a journey, but rarely of death as an act of communion. For some the journey is rich and colorful. For others, life is a confusing affair, too opaque to admit the possibility of purpose. For them, if life is a journey, it is one without direction or meaning. My own kaleidoscope of experience comes into focus through the lens of faith. I choose to live my life in relationship with the God who has revealed himself in Jesus Christ. This has cultivated in me a sense of traveling home to God. I face my mortality in the conviction that death is not extinction, but the gateway to the fulfillment of human life. God turns my existence into life, and my life into a pilgrimage.

As a result, the fears that haunt me are more about the process of dying than the event itself. Dying is not the issue. It is living until I die. I endeavor to entrust the past to God's mercy, the present to his grace, and the future to his providence. Shortly before he died Augustine wrote of his longing for God: "There we shall be still and see; we shall see and we shall love; we shall love and we shall praise. Behold what will be, in the end that has no end."[31] Seeing God is true contentment, the goal of human striving, the resolution of human restlessness. There is no possibility of boredom in the "end that has no end," only an experience of deepening love. Faith does not devalue this life, but places it on a surer foundation and in an eternal perspective. Which is why I warm to Boethius's words, written in the sixth century:

To see thee is the end and the beginning. Thou carriest us, and thou dost go before us. Thou art the journey, and the journey's end.[32]

REFLECTION

Are there things that I need to let go of?

Luther said, "If I knew that I was going to die tomorrow, I would plant a tree today." If I knew I were going to die tomorrow, what would I do today?

What epitaph would I like written on my tombstone?

God be in my head,

and in my understanding;

God be in mine eyes,

and in my looking;

God be in my mouth,

and in my speaking;

God be in my heart,

and in my loving;

God be at mine end,

and at my departing.

FROM *THE SARUM PRIMER* (1514)

Notes

1. T. S. Eliot, "East Coker," IV, *Four Quartets,* in *The Complete Poems and Plays of T. S. Eliot* (London: Faber and Faber, 1940), 182.

2. Richard Needham, *Toronto Globe and Mail.*

3. Philip Larkin, "Toads," *The Less Deceived* (London: The Marvell Press, 1955), 32.

4. Philip Larkin, "Toads Revisited," *The Whitsun Weddings* (London: Faber and Faber, 1971), 18.

5. Augustine, *Confessions,* I, 1.

6. Augustine, *Confessions,* X, 8.

7. Andreas Huyssen famously described contemporary Western culture as a "culture of amnesia" in *Twilight Memories: Marking Time in a Culture of Amnesia* (London: Routledge, 1955).

8. See Jonathan Sacks, *The Dignity of Difference: How to Avoid the Clash of Civilizations* (London, New York and Sydney: Continuum, 2002), 178.

9. Neil Belton, *The Good Listener* (London: Phoenix, 1999), 25–6.

10. Aeschylus, *Agamemnon*, 176–83.

11. Evelyn Underhill, "For Wholeness," source unknown.

12. *King Lear*, Act V, scene 3.

13. Interview, "Midweek," Radio 4, BBC, Wednesday 6 October 2010.

14. Interview of Frances Lawrence by James Naughtie, "The Today Programme," Radio 4, BBC, Tuesday 21 August 2007.

15. Matthew uses the word *opheleimata* (Matt. 6:12), meaning "that which is owing." He is interested in the ordering of the Christian community and in the settling of grievances. It is from Matthew that we have the parable of the Unmerciful Steward who refuses to help his fellow servant and mitigate his debts. Luke uses the word *hamartias*, meaning "sin," (Luke 11:4). He celebrates the way sinners are entering the kingdom of God ahead of so-called righteous people. It is from Luke that we have the parable of the Prodigal Son and the story of the penitent thief crucified beside Jesus.

16. R. S. Thomas, "Self-Portrait," *Laboratories of the Spirit* (London: Macmillan, 1975), 27.

17. Gregory of Nyssa, Homily 2 *"On the Song of Songs."*

18. *Noverim te, Domine, noverim me.* Augustine, *On the Trinity,* IX, 18.

19. R. S. Thomas, 1978, "Pilgrimages," *Frequencies* (London, Macmillan, 1978), 51.

20. Viktor Frankl's own free translation of Kierkegaard's statement:

    "Alas, fortune's door does not open inward so that one can push it open by rushing at it, but it opens outward, and therefore one can do nothing about it." *Søren Kierkegaard, Either/Or,* trans. Howard Hong and Edna Hong (Princeton, NJ: Princeton University Press, 1987), 23.

21. William Law, *A Serious Call to a Devout and Holy Life.*

22. W. H. Auden, "In memory of W. B. Yeats," *Collected Shorter Poems 1927–1957* (London: Faber and Faber, 1966).

23. Francis de Sales, *Introduction to a Devout Life,* III, 10.

24. *Autarkeia, e.g. Stoicorum Veterum Fragmenta,* coll. J. Arnim, III, 1903–24, p. 67,3; p. 68,5; Democritus, 246; Hippocrates, Ep. 17.

25. Jean-Pierre de Caussade, *Abandonment to Divine Providence,* VI, 5.

26. See Albert Jewell (ed.), *Spirituality and Ageing* (London: Jessica Kingsley Publishers, 1999), 9–13; Jewell, *Ageing, Spirituality and Well-being* (London: Jessica Kingsley Publishers, 2004), 11–26.

27. *Vacate, et videte quoniam ego sum Deus.*

28. Bronnie West, Ezine Articles.

29. Dylan Thomas, "Do not go gentle into that good night," *Collected Poems 1934–1952* (London: J. M. Dent & Sons, 1952), 116.

30. Pierre Teilhard de Chardin, *Le Milieu Divin*, Paris; ET 1960 (London: Collins & Sons, 1957), 69–70.

31. Augustine, *City of God*, XXII, 30.

32. Attributed to Boethius, *Consolations of Philosophy.*

Acknowledgments

The Author and Publisher are grateful for permission to reproduce material under copyright, and would be grateful to be informed of any omissions or inaccuracies in this respect. They are particularly grateful to the following copyright holders:

David Higham Associates for an extract from Dylan Thomas's poem "Do not go gentle into that good night," *Collected Poems 1934–1952*.

Faber and Faber for an extract from T. S. Eliot, *Four Quartets*.

Johnson & Alcock Ltd, for permission to reproduce Jenny Joseph's poem "When I am old I shall wear purple."

The Estate of R. S. Thomas, for an extract from the poem "Self-Portrait."

Macmillan Publishers Ltd, for an extract from R. S. Thomas's poem "Pilgrimages," originally published in *Frequencies* (London: Macmillan, 1978) and reprinted in *Collected Poems 1945-1990* (London, Phoenix, 1966).

The Wylie Agency for an extract from W. H. Auden's poem "In Memory of W. B. Yeats," *Collected Shorter Poems 1927–1957.*

ABOUT PARACLETE PRESS

Who We Are

Paraclete Press is a publisher of books, recordings, and DVDs on Christian spirituality. Our publishing represents a full expression of Christian belief and practice—from Catholic to Evangelical, from Protestant to Orthodox.

We are the publishing arm of the Community of Jesus, an ecumenical monastic community in the Benedictine tradition. As such, we are uniquely positioned in the marketplace without connection to a large corporation and with informal relationships to many branches and denominations of faith.

What We Are Doing

BOOKS / Paraclete publishes books that show the richness and depth of what it means to be Christian. Although Benedictine spirituality is at the heart of all that we do, we publish books that reflect the Christian experience across many cultures, time periods, and houses of worship. We publish books that nourish the vibrant life of the church and its people—books about spiritual practice, formation, history, ideas, and customs.

We have several different series, including the best-selling Paraclete Essentials and Paraclete Giants series of classic texts in contemporary English; A Voice from the Monastery—men and women monastics writing about living a spiritual life today; award-winning poetry; best-selling gift books for children on the occasions of baptism and first communion; and the Active Prayer Series that brings creativity and liveliness to any life of prayer.

RECORDINGS / From Gregorian chant to contemporary American choral works, our music recordings celebrate sacred choral music through the centuries. Paraclete distributes the recordings of the internationally acclaimed choir Gloriæ Dei Cantores, praised for their "rapt and fathomless spiritual intensity" by *American Record Guide*, and the Gloriæ Dei Cantores Schola, which specializes in the study and performance of Gregorian chant. Paraclete is also the exclusive North American distributor of the recordings of the Monastic Choir of St. Peter's Abbey in Solesmes, France, long considered to be a leading authority on Gregorian chant.

VIDEOS / Our videos offer spiritual help, healing, and biblical guidance for life issues: grief and loss, marriage, forgiveness, anger management, facing death, and spiritual formation.

Learn more about us at our website:
www.paracletepress.com,
or call us toll-free at 1-800-451-5006.

SCAN TO READ MORE

You may also be interested in...

Small Surrenders:
A Lenten Journey
Emilie Griffin

"Griffin is a trustworthy guide. . . . She writes with the unmistakable authenticity and authority of a woman steeped in prayer." —*America*

Join Emilie Griffin in this daily companion for the Lenten journey. Using ancient and modern texts as inspiration for her own reflections, Emilie Griffin nurtures and guides us into a deeper knowledge of ourselves and God. We discover that Lent is our chance for a fresh start, and an opportunity to joyfully put ourselves in God's hands.

ISBN 978-1-55725-642-3
$16.99, Paperback

Praying in Color:
Drawing a New Path
to God
Sybil MacBeth

Already in its
5th printing

If you are word-weary, stillness-challenged, easily distracted, or just in need of a new way to pray, give "praying in color" a try. Sybil MacBeth introduces a simple, creative, joy-filled prayer practice.

"Just as Julia Cameron in *The Artist's Way* showed the hardened Harvard businessman he had a creative artist lurking within, MacBeth makes it astonishingly clear that anyone with a box of colors and some paper can have a conversation with God. Readers of all ages, experience and religions will find this a fresh, invigorating and even exhilarating way to spend time with themselves and their Creator." —*Publishers Weekly*

ISBN: 978-1-55725-512-9
$16.95, Paperback